How I Got RICH Doing What I LOVE!

Dr BOIKANYO TRUST PHENYO

Copyright © 2019 Dr Boikanyo Trust Phenyo

All rights reserved.

ISBN-13: 978-1-9806-0883-7

DEDICATION

For my dear mother.
You raised me well, thank you.

CONTENTS

	Acknowledgments	i
	Forward by Lance Greenfield	ii
	Introduction	1
	Part 1: About me	
1	My family	3
2	My school years	7
3	My working years	10
	Part 2: My Massage	
4	Preparing for a session	13
5	During a session	16
6	My technique/style	18
7	Finishing off a session	22
	Part 3: My Clients	
8	Client testimonials	24
	Part 4: My Passions	
9	Dancing	28
10	Modelling (including biographical photos)	32
	Part 5: You can get Rich too!	
11	Work on your dreams	46
	a) Getting rich is an inside job	46
	b) Set you goals	47
	c) Consistency is key	47
	d) The secret of living rich	48
	Part 6: What do experts say?	
12	Quotes from successful people	49
	Part 7: Resources	
	My videos	54
	Books I have read	54
	About the author	58
	Notes	61

ACKNOWLEDGMENTS

Thanks to everyone who made this book possible. **Janusz Miarka** for listening and encouraging me. **Philip Wake** for reading and editing my work. My beautiful daughter **Katrinah Phenyo** for all her sacrifices and being patient with me. **My brothers** for all their love, therefore, they will always have a special place in my heart. I would also like to thank my best friend **Setshego Olebile** for naturally being my accountability partner. A huge thanks to all my mentors: **Sheena Walker, Edward J C Smith, Justina Mutale, Hannah B. Lecha, Gagan Arora, Nicholas J Reynolds** and **Lance Greenfield.**

FOREWORD BY LANCE GREENFIELD
(Author of Eleven Miles and Knitting Can Walk)

My grandmother was an incredibly insightful woman. There was a day when she inspired me with one of the wisest pieces of wisdom that I have ever heard. She imparted the true meaning and origin of the word 'wealth.'

It was on a day when I was bemoaning the unfairness of how much wealthier some people were than others. She was unimpressed by my undisguised envy.

"Do you know the real meaning of the word, 'wealth'?"

"Yes. Of course!" I replied. "A wealthy person is one who own many expensive possessions and has lots of money."

"No, Lance. You couldn't be more wrong. The word is a combination of 'well-being' and 'good health.' If you are not healthy and you aren't happy with your life, it doesn't matter how much money you have or how many possessions you own, you cannot be wealthy."

When you think about it. This is very true.

By my grandmother's definition, Boikanyo Trust Phenyo is one of the wealthiest women I have ever known. Not only that, but she is also incredibly generous. In this book, she shares with us the reasons that she has become so wealthy, doing the things that she loves. She is happy. She is healthy. And so, she is wealthy.

Boikanyo tells us how, despite the financially poor background of her family and the village in the Okavango Delta region of Botswana, she considers herself to be rich. When you read her words of wisdom, you will agree and your own life will be enriched.

I have been personally inspired by this awesome and admirable woman, who was the driving force behind the heroine of my first novel, Eleven Miles. When you have read this book, you will also possess the knowledge to become rich, doing what you love.

INTRODUCTION

I have always been rich! Even though I come from a financially poor background, deep down I have always been rich. I have only just realized how rich I have been, all the way from my childhood to my adulthood.

But before this, I used to create poverty in my mind because I had a poor mindset and focused on all the negative things around me. To my surprise, looking back and counting all my blessings, I can see all the positive side of my life. I had everything, but I never realized how lucky I was!

I did not use my creative mind to see the many opportunities around me that I could easily have pursued. I had loving parents, lots of brothers and a beautiful sister. All I had to do was believe in myself and feel good about all that was going for me.

My talent had always been there, and I knew this, but I did not realize that that was all I needed to be happy! I love and appreciate my job now. It's amazing to see the perfect balance I now have in my life. Finally I love my life and feel rich because I now know that everything starts with me, with loving myself. I know how to create a happier richer life for myself.

I spend quality time with myself. I have created what I call My Life Wheel (see the diagram below), which I regularly update. It's a wonderful way of monitoring my progress.

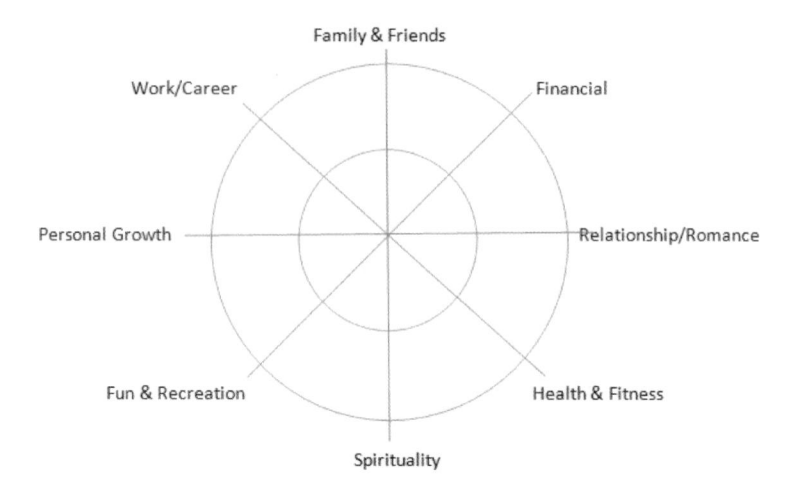

```
                    Family & Friends
        Work/Career     |     Financial
                  \     |     /
                   \    |    /
                    \   |   /
Personal Growth ─────●───── Relationship/Romance
                    /   |   \
                   /    |    \
                  /     |     \
       Fun & Recreation |  Health & Fitness
                    Spirituality
```

I give each area a score from 0 to 10 (0 is closest to center and means not satisfied and 10 is closest to outer edge and means totally satisfied). Each month I pick the area with the lowest score and then think of ways or actions to take to increase this score. This works wonders, and I challenge you to try it.

This book is about using your passion to generate income. I will be drawing from my experiences and how I finally discovered what I really enjoy and feel blessed to do every day. I love giving as well as receiving a massage.

When I am in the massage room, I feel happy. There is peace in my head. I feel like this is what I have been called here on Earth to do. Somehow my head becomes clear. If I had any problem or worry, this is where all my questions get answered.

When I was young, my dad used to ask us kids to massage his feet after his long hours of work during the day. He loved being touched and he would fall asleep. My mum and my auntie used to ask us to walk on their back and it was all fun for us. From an early age, I appreciated the power of touch. I can recall as far back as when I was a baby that I enjoyed my mum gently stroking my body. Her touch was like magic and could easily send me to sleep.

Now as an adult I have learnt from her that she gave all her babies regular massages after a bath. It was something her mother taught her. Touching is the most basic of human impulses and massage is a therapeutic extension of touching dating back to ancient times.

Today, the therapeutic value of massage is being recognized. It is regaining its rightful place in health care as complementary to other medical treatments, and as a means of helping all of us to maintain positive health.

PART 1: ABOUT ME

1 MY FAMILY

I come from a big family. Mum and dad had eight children. My two sisters passed away leaving only six: me and 5 brothers. Both sisters were younger than me. One passed away when she was a baby, so I don't remember her as I was also very young. The other sister left us in her teens. I remember her very well. She was very bright at school, a real genius, and I loved her very much. She was generously loving with a beautiful soul but sadly she got stabbed to death by a jealous boyfriend after a night out together just before he committed suicide.

I was the first person to go to University from my family. I remember working very hard at school as I wanted to get a better job so that I could help my family, especially my mum.

My father is a typical African man: as head of the family, he has the final say in everything and his wife & kids must obey him at all times . . . and so on. He had a good job as an operator in the diamond mines of Orapa & Letlhakane. He was a good-looking man who drove fast cars and couldn't help attracting lots of girls who he was pleased to entertain. He did not allow my mum to work as she was just meant to be a housewife who looked after the children.

However, because I grew up in a Christian family, people often thought our family was perfect. My dad was a pastor in the church, so we went to church every Sunday. My parents have always been friendly, outgoing, people so our house was always full of visitors.

My mum never had enough money to feed or clothe us properly despite her husband having a well-paid job. She did everything she could with what she was given to look after us as well as she could. I watched her cry sometimes. She taught us to pray and prayed with us particularly when we didn't have anything to eat.

My dad was always away. We missed him a lot because he was hardly ever there. When he was home he would call my mum stupid and find a way to go out somewhere rather than stay at home with her. He compared her with all the women he spent time with. He complained that she couldn't cook as perfectly, she couldn't clean or iron as well as other women. Even now in retirement he keeps his pension to himself and doesn't show any respect for her.

When he was not well, he expected her to be a superwoman and do every little thing for him, but he wouldn't do the same for her. He said my mum is uneducated and can't reason yet I have discovered she is one of the wisest people I know! She has logic and can reason far better than he can. My mother told us that she was very bright at school. She loved studying and could have done very well. Unfortunately, she was taken out of school before completing her primary education because a marriage had been arranged for her. Her father removed her from school and handed her over to her future husband and his family without a thought for her own wellbeing. She was taught to respect her husband, obey him without question and accept anything he did including abuse. Men were head of the family, so their words were always final!

As I was growing up, I became more and more confused. My dad was a very good pastor at church, yet he was not good to my mum. He was very good to everyone else except her. Thank God, he never laid hands on us kids and neither did he on mum. His abuse was always emotional rather than physical.

Our childhood was not a good environment for all of us kids to grow up in at all. My mum decided to stay in Maun while my dad worked and stayed in Orapa, and now I understand why. He used to visit whenever he had mini holidays from work. I grew up with my mum and completed all my school years in Maun, so I only visited my father during school holidays. All my younger siblings stayed with him so went to school in Orapa.

Each time I visited, they would report to me how my father mistreated them or how they would go on for days without food. You see, even though our father had a well-paid job, most of his salary was not spent on his family but on other people so there was never enough food in the house.

I remember one day when I got home my sister tried to tell me how hard it was as she was the only girl in the house when mum and I were not there. Instead of words coming out of her mouth a lot of tears came streaming down her face. I was heartbroken. Somehow, my father had always treated me differently from everyone else in the family. This is because I was named after his mother and he used to call me mum. He was much nicer to me most of the time and would listen to me when I questioned him.

Because it was not his way to beat or lay hands on my brothers and sister, he used to punish them in so many cruel ways. He would starve them giving them no food at home after school or lock the house so they could not get in. I thought all these things were so cruel. Buying them new things including clothes was a rare occurrence. My mum would buy them some things with the little money he would give her or the money she earned from the mini-businesses she used to run to help herself.

Being a smart woman, my mother enrolled in an adult learning course and learnt how to sew. She learnt how to make beautiful dresses, skirts, tops and jackets. My father would become jealous every time she seemed to be making progress and he would take all her savings! She baked delicious fat cakes (like doughnuts) at home and sold them. Again, he would come and destroy everything to discourage her as much as he could. She was not allowed to learn how to drive a car: perhaps because he was afraid she would run away . . . I cannot be sure.

I was angry with my father for many years but now I have learnt to let it go. I have learnt to forgive him for I will never understand his model of the world, his reasons for doing what he did and continues to do. Anger has a way of backfiring if it cannot be resolved, so letting it go is always the best course to take.

We were discouraged to speak up against our parents. We never raised our voices even though we were hurting inside. Seeing my family this way, I decided to work very hard at school so that I could change my mother's future and make her smile again.

Dad with me & one of my brothers

Dad with one of my brothers

Mum and me

Mum and Dad

Mum and me

2 MY SCHOOL YEARS

From an early age, I was very competitive at school. I was an athlete who enjoyed running and loved winning all my races because it made me feel good.

I had a teacher at primary school who used to beat me up every time I arrived late in the morning. I did not like this very much, so it seemed natural to me to avoid this by running to school and that's why I became so good at running I suppose. My house was about 11 miles from school. My brother and I had to wake up very very early as we had a long journey ahead of us. Most of the time we had to go to school without breakfast as there was not much food at home.

Interestingly enough, we never had an alarm clock to wake us up because my mum always managed to wake us up on time without one! When she heard our cockcrow outside our hut she knew that it was time to get up. It never failed!

We lived in our lovely hut which my mum built with her very own hands. I remember when I was between 10 and 15 years old that I helped her build it. We fetched mud and cow dung a few miles away and carried it on our heads. We fetched water from the river every day. I knew how to balance a bucket full of water on my head: proud moments in my life I will never forget!

There was no electricity in our homes during those days, so we used candles and paraffin lamps. I did my studies: reading and writing all my homework under a candle light or during the day.

At Junior Secondary school I was always in the top 3 overall in all my subjects. If I didn't get position 1, it would invariably be 2 or 3. I loved doing well at school. It made my mum happy and I collected lots of presents at prize giving. Due to my academic excellence, I was selected to be in the first chess club at our school. An expatriate teacher from Germany taught us chess and it was fascinating. We didn't know what the game was, but he made it so interesting. We mastered the game, competed with other schools outside Maun and our team did well. When Softball was introduced at school, I was one of the first people to join. I loved running already, so this game was perfect for me. I was placed as a short stop; always running around ... so refreshing.

I travelled around the country with my school teams. If it wasn't academic such as Science and Maths fairs, it would be extra-curricular activities like chess, softball or athletics. My mum loved packing my bags and preparing my packed food for each trip. She didn't have to give me much, bless her, because the school took care of us. The thrill of going on these trips was amazing. I could see how proud my mum was and my heart was filled with love.

One day I wrote something like this in my journal: "The suffering of my family is one of the best ways to help me realize that I need to work hard in school so that I can change our future for the better." This paragraph is still engraved in my sub-conscious mind and I know that it has helped me to do as well as I have.

I went on to Senior Secondary school where I continued to do very well. As an overall high achiever across my subjects, I was selected along with other students to do pure sciences (Triple science – Biology, Chemistry & Physics). Again, my competitive side kicked in. I became captain in the girl's athletic team, represented my school in the chess club and joined the debating team. I passed my BGCSE (Botswana General Certificate of Secondary Education) with flying colours. In fact out of a class of about 40 students, only I and one boy achieved first class. So many proud moments to remember for a lifetime!

After our BGCSE exams, we were all expected to do Tirelo Sechaba (National Service) for a full year. We had to travel to different villages, live with different families and learn their ways of doing things. I was posted to the furthest end of the country, a village called Kanye about 1,500km away from Maun. I was posted in a primary school as an assistant teacher. I fell in love with teaching because the little ones were so cute. I joined the school ballroom dancing club and the music was great. I was serving with two other friends at this school. One boy was my former classmate from senior school and the other was from the same village of Kanye. Somehow this boy got away with refusing to be sent to any place far away because he fancied staying close to his family! I thought to myself that he was stupid. How could anyone refuse to take full advantage of the adventure of being in a new place far away from where you have lived all your life? The government really did everything for us and looked after us so well. Transport was provided to take us to our destinations safely, accommodation was organized and there were always plenty of families ready to welcome us in their homes. Getting paid every month was a bonus and it really was exciting. We missed home, yes, but the experience prepared us for the corporate world and we got to think about our future careers.

I went to the University of Botswana shortly after the National Service. I chose Bachelor of Science (BSc) for my degree. During my final years, I majored in Physics and was the only girl taking Physics with the boys. I loved competing with boys. I valued my education very much, so I stayed focused, keeping away from distracting activities.

I had a solid plan. I was going to get married first before having kids. Unfortunately, during my last year at Uni an idiot tricked me, got me pregnant and ran away. Anyway, that's another story! I have totally let it go and forgiven him now.

I had a burning desire to do well, I envisioned myself running a successful business one day. I completed my BSc degree, then went on to do Postgraduate Diploma in Education (PGDE) majoring in Physics and Maths.

Me at the University of Botswana (UB)

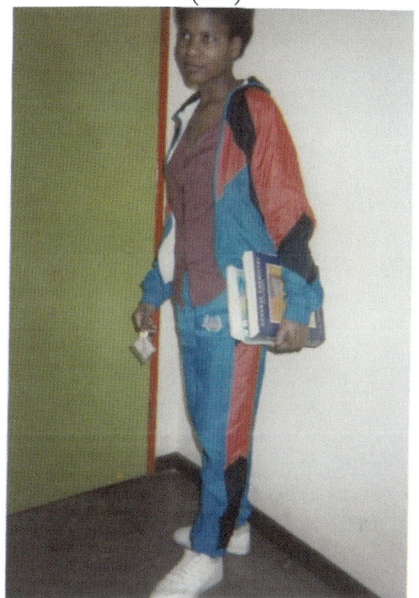

Science club BSc students at UB

3 MY WORKING YEARS

My first job was as a Physics teacher at Letlhakane Senior Secondary School. I was shortly promoted to Physics Coordinator which was nice. I met my Irish partner here. After 2 years he decided to go back to London where he was based before going to Botswana. I naturally followed him shortly after he left.

When I arrived in London, everything was different: a cultural shock. I had never seen so many people in one place and everyone seemed to be in a rush, ignoring everyone else . . . OMG!

A few months later I went back home to process my residence visa as I couldn't do any type of work without it. I came back and started working as a teacher. I enjoyed it at first but as time went on it became more and more challenging. I was teaching both Science and Physics to secondary school students ranging from 11 to 18 years olds (GCSE and A levels). I met very tough and challenging students from rough areas of London. I found myself just about managing their behaviour in the classroom let alone teaching them. I got more and more discouraged. I lost my confidence and eventually lost interest in being a teacher.

I blamed my lack of interest to a lot of things: for example, my subject Physics is a mathematical science and most students were generally not interested in science particularly the girls. I blamed the school system, head teachers, student behaviour and work load. I moved from one school to another hoping to make a fresh start, but still had the same problems. In the end I quit, blaming everything but myself but I now realize that classroom teaching was simply not my passion.

I tried office work as a financial administrator for a year. This was by far the worst job I had ever done! It was dead easy, not at all challenging and I couldn't stand being ordered about. That really was not for me. I valued my freedom, my individuality and my ability to get on with my work without being pushed.

I thought hard about what I really wanted to do. Ideally, I wanted to have a home-based business and enjoy what I am doing. One day I went to get my hair done and the hairdresser was operating from home so that she could look after her two young kids while she was working. She had turned her garage into an office so she could not only do people's hair but also run a mini-shop selling hair products. This gave me an idea: how wonderful would it be to do something similar? However, I am rubbish at doing hair so couldn't do that. At this time I was working as a voluntary trained counsellor at Reading Pregnancy Crisis Centre. I was working with experienced counsellors helping young teens who found themselves pregnant unexpectedly. We helped them to find the available options and make decisions best for them. I was already used to working with young people, so I found this enjoyable, but I needed to make money and be happy with what I was doing at the same time.

I wanted to do something that I would really enjoy, so my mind began searching for possibilities. A light bulb moment - MASSAGE - bingo! If I re-trained, I could be a Massage Therapist. I did some research and found out I could either do this at home or travel to my clients' locations. Massage is science based (biology), so it would be easy for me to learn besides I love giving as well as receiving a massage. It made sense, so I invested in re-training.

I started working from home and I loved it. I got great reviews and people came back for more and more. The first time in my treatment room, it felt peaceful. I enjoyed the silence, oh so different from the classroom noise. Happy days!

I did more courses in Massage Therapy, so I could improve my techniques and provide a better-quality service. I did some healing courses and now my conventional massage techniques are mixed with healing techniques making my particular massage service unique. The more I did this work, the more I loved it. My counselling skills came in handy for some of my clients who needed emotional as well as physical healing and I decided to offer counselling sessions as well as massage sessions.

I now consider myself a Lifestyle Specialist: I work with people who want to improve their lifestyles, through relaxation (massage), healthy eating (diet & nutrition), fitness (yoga & exercise) and counselling (mostly relationship).

With my students at Letlhakane Senior Secondary School (LSSS)

With my students in the Physics Lab at LSSS

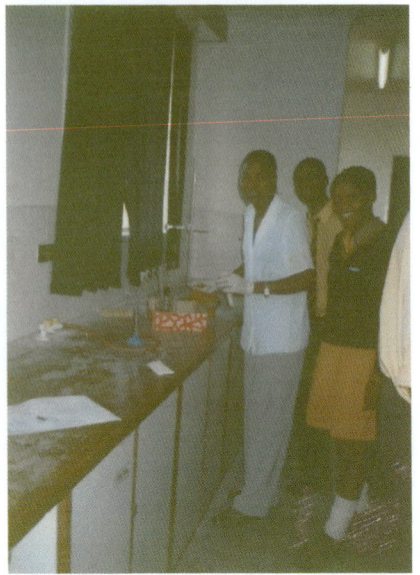

PART 2: MY MASSAGE

4 PREPARING FOR A SESSION

Massage Therapy is a job I could do whether I got paid or not, so I am very fortunate getting paid for what I love doing! Happy moments!

During my training I was advised to limit my clients to a maximum of 5 per day at an hour each. I discovered I could handle even 10 clients per day without getting tired! I get excited and am passionate about what I do, valuing each and every moment I spend with my clients. I therefore aim to provide the best service I can. I have been doing this for over 7 years now and each day it gets more and more exciting. The good feedback I get from my clients gives me all the courage and the excitement to do more and to want to provide more.

Here is how I get ready for my massage sessions:

Before I go into my treatment room, I already have good intentions for my client. I say a quiet prayer of petition in the vein of: divine intelligence, heal my client, make him feel good, use my hands to transfer good energy and let any negative or bad energy flow out or get drained back to mother earth where it came from. I wear a genuine smile, greet my client with happiness and re-assure him that he is in good hands.

A therapist needs to be neat, clean and professional always. I make sure my room is tidy and clean with everything I need in its rightful place before I begin. I must visit the bathroom and wash my hands. Hygiene is very important to me, so I encourage my clients to have a quick shower before we start. This way we both have a good experience as this is as much for me as it is for them. My treatment room must encourage a good experience for my clients. I keep smelly things like food out of the room and burn relaxing aromatic candles with oils of essence.

It is very important for me to stay hydrated, so I usually have a glass of water just in case. I believe water has healing qualities, so this makes sure I am in a good state, have good intentions and am feeling grateful. As water enters my body with good vibrations from my thoughts, these get translated back to the person who need it most: my client. I also provide a glass of water with sliced lemon for my clients before and after the session as the client's body undergoes a detox process during the massage. Therefore, excess waste need to be flushed out afterwards.

I encourage doing all the talking or discussions before or after the session as I prefer the sound of silence during the massage.

I like to know a little bit about my clients, so I get to know them by asking a few leading questions. Usually they open up about why they need massage therapy. I make mental notes because I prefer not to take notes in front of them to ensure they believe that what they say to me is totally confidential. Each client is given a code name before they arrive. I record whatever I have gathered during the session after they had left. I make little notes for myself about their needs and what they are suffering from.

Some people do not like their bellies massaged for example or they might have skin allergies, so I get to discover these little issues before we begin the first session and make notes later so that I don't have to ask again as it is important that the client feels on subsequent visits that I remember them well. I also explain to them how I work, what to expect and what I expect from them.

Massage has profound effects on our health. It improves circulation, relaxes muscles, aids digestion and, by stimulating the lymphatic system it speeds up the elimination of waste products.

My first treatment room

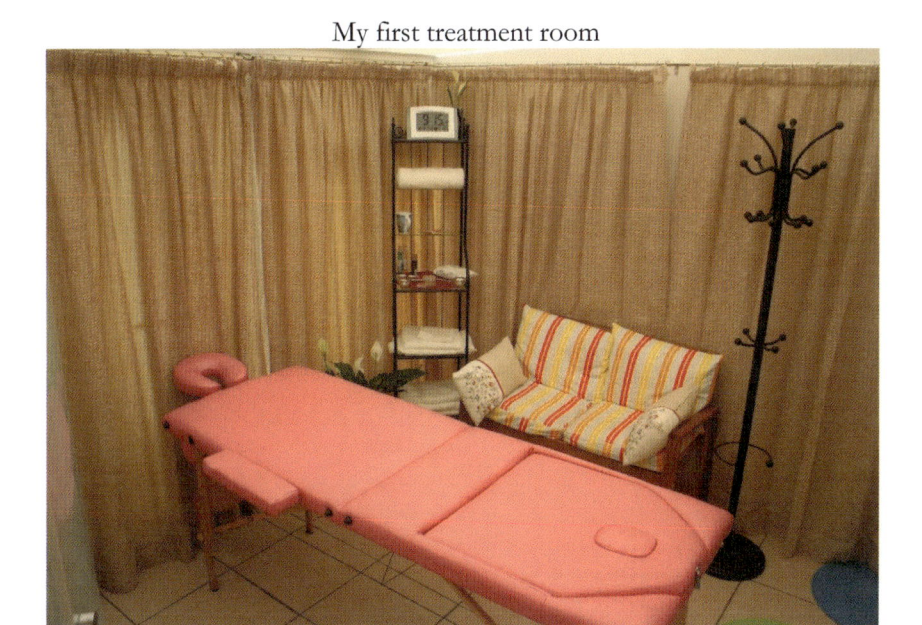

5 DURING A SESSION

During the massage, I encourage silence as I work best this way. I communicate with my higher self to enable me to reach my highest potential. I do my work in a meditative state. That way I tap into the infinite power within me and everything becomes possible. My hands can trace and feel my client's ailments. I can feel the energy exchange. I find it easier to feel and open my client's main healing points (Chakras) if I use whole-body movement as I massage.

I develop a rapport with my client through breathing. We synchronize and end up breathing in and out at the same time. When this happens, I know that the client is relaxed, and healing is taking place.

Massage is as much beneficial to me as it is to my clients. I feel energized, relaxed and happier after each session. This is because I work with energy. Coming from Quantum Physics background everything makes sense! Our world is particulate in nature and everything is made up of tiny particles. We are all connected. We send out vibrations to each other and, when you are aware as much as I am, everything is fascinating. It is amazing what we can achieve through our thoughts.

I have had some clients literally crying after our session. Some just lie there numb for a while. They can't explain or express the experience as they had never felt this way before.

I make sure I am totally relaxed throughout, and I encourage my clients to do the same. The easiest way for them to relax is to take deep slow breaths from the diaphragm as this will encourage all the muscles of their body to relax.

Some people fall into a deep sleep. This is ok because it allows me to work with their energy more effectively. I work on opening their main chakras until I can feel or sense a bright steady flow of clean energy. When there is a blockage, I can usually sense a dark spot or not-so-clear energy. Naturally I would focus for a while on this spot until it is cleared. In most cases a few more sessions with the client will be required. To be honest, I do not always need my client to tell me what their problems are because I can feel or sense them during the massage, but some people prefer to tell me so that they can be sure that I will concentrate on the areas they are worried about.

I had a client who remained on the massage table for more than half an hour after the massage because he just couldn't move! He enjoyed the massage so very much it was an entirely new and different experience for him. It's a good thing I always give myself plenty of time in between clients to allow both of us time for full recovery.

There is a healing energy circulating in the room during my massage sessions. I can feel the love radiating from me to my client, to the Source and then back to me and my client. I love working with energy because I feel enlightened and wonderful. It's the best feeling ever. Exciting moments!

Once I arrive in this place, everything is possible. Answers to all my problems are revealed and I am always grateful. Because I love what I do, I have everything I need.

I like to think that I have magic fingers, as I work my fingers through my client's body. I can feel where all their tension or ailments are. I am guided by infinite intelligence to touch the right points, where the body need it most. This often brings out emotions, feelings of satisfaction and gratitude. There is magic in the power of touch and I am happy and grateful to be a medium between the client and the Source (the Source of all energy).

It is so much easier to do what you love. I feel rich indeed. Each day I carry out my work with pride as I know that the Universe has got my back. I am safe, secure and protected, I am at one with the Source – the one that has always been and always will be.

I get chatty clients sometimes. I understand they may be nervous or that some people find it hard to relax so talking helps ease their nerves, but this can massively break the flow of energy! With practice I have mastered the skill of concentration. I can easily get back to my focus anytime I want. When I first started, being interrupted created a sort of imbalance or instability but these days it's smooth all the way through.

The temperature must be just right for both of us in the room. The air must be clean so that we have plenty of oxygen to breath. We must both breath properly: deeply without strain. This is where we get in touch with our higher selves. We can tap into the infinite power of the universe. It's a wonderful feeling.

The experiences that my client receives, I receive also, therefore the therapy benefits both of us equally. I feel refreshed, energized and happy. This is what true fulfillment is all about.

6 MY TECHNIQUE/STYLE

My massage is based on Swedish Techniques which includes the use of aromatherapy. I use different essential oils for different treatments or moods. I believe very much in alternative therapy. Our body has been designed so that it is capable of healing itself. Massage with a combination of essential oils can solve all kinds of stress related problems.

I have noticed so many positive changes since I started working with my clients. A lot of them can do more and enjoy life better because of the quality of the service I provide. Most keep coming back for more and I very much appreciate them every time they do. Every day this makes me stronger and stronger and makes me feel that I too can provide more.

One of the reasons why I do not get tired very easily when I do my work is that I use light strokes and concentrate on the soft tissues just below the surface rather that hard or deep tissues. Also, I work with energy which means less physical work.

My style is more relaxing than invigorating. I use long, slow strokes with plenty of aromatherapy oils. My strength is light or soft, never hard. I find this better and easier because I can go on for a long time without getting tired. I use a simple method: I transfer my body weight to aid in the energy transfer which provides rhythm and depth to my technique.

Most of my clients also prefer this style. Providing the client has regular massage sessions with me, it is more effective than deep tissue massage which is more likely to cause damage than provide an appropriate cure.

I make sure I eat well: eating only unprocessed food for example. I exercise every day, doing simple yoga movements for about 10 minutes. Sometimes I do a little jogging which I really enjoy as I am after all a former athlete. Keeping myself fit and healthy ensures I can deliver a good service.

A new client booked a session for 1.5 hours. I was happy he chose a longer time with me because it is an indication of someone who values the benefits of a massage. We started ok, but about 20minutes in to the massage he said:

"Can we just stop this please? I am not feeling this. Your massage feels mediocre. I have had much better!"

I was not offended. In fact, I respected his feelings, so I gave him his money back.

I appreciate that my style is not for everyone. I totally get that. I am grateful, regardless, and thank God and the Universe for this opportunity. In life there is no way you are going to please everybody. You must just be true to yourself. Keep doing what gives you joy and joyous things will come back to you. Love everything and everybody and the Universe will give you back even more love. We are all connected by a universal source of energy which radiates back whatever frequency we put into it.

I have discovered that the best way for me to get either in or out of tune (with the positive or negative respectively) is to meditate. I have learnt to quiet my mind and be at one with the power within. I meditate before and after sessions. I stay in the meditative mode throughout massage sessions.

As I work with both positive and negative energy, it is very important for me to identify and separate the two. I am able to do this by understanding where my energy level is in the first place. I start with being grounded, being calm and letting go of all the negative emotions. I then go through the process of asking the Source to help my client go through the same on their behalf. I send a prayer of petition to the infinite power, allowing a positive flow of energy. Any negative energy coming towards me I believe is cast aside by my spirit guides who are at work with me always. I am safe secure and protected.

Usually when clients come with negative energy, I will send them away if I feel I can't help them. This might take the form of excuses like: "I can't afford your service", "I prefer a different style", and so on. I just know the kind of people I am can work with and it makes my life so much easier only to work with those people. Good follows good because energy follows thoughts. My thoughts manifests everything that I want which is awesome!

In the main, I attract only the best clients to work with. I communicate with my guides through my thoughts and they do the same. Our frequencies must match for us to understand each other. I love working with them and I thank them every day. What I really and truly appreciate is the way they are always available every time I need them without fail. They are experts at what they do and I am just a channel.

I pray every day to be as clear a channel as possible for my clients and for my guides. For energy of the Source to reach my client, I must bring it to them through my positively guided intentions. When my client reaches a stage where they can access this super power, all things are possible, and all their ailments can be healed.

As much as our body is capable of healing itself, we must relax and allow the flow of healing energy. Lying still, totally relaxed, allows a smooth flow of this healing energy with all the healing points open and we can feel better.

When clients come to me with an uneasy or unrelaxed state, as soon as they enter my aura, it automatically calms them down and their energy level increases, enabling me to help them.

Each therapist is different. We are all individuals and use different styles. I tell my students that what works for me might not work for them, but it's important to learn all styles before you develop your unique way of doing things.

I like starting with the back because that helps me get connected to clients as this is the largest area of their body. I can do all sorts of strokes and pressures. By the time I finish the whole back, more than half of the time allocated has passed and the client has fully relaxed and have got used to my touch. Moving to the front, I attend to all the body parts then finish off with a head massage. Most people doze off at this stage. The client needs a few minutes before gently awakening.

I have used my athletic background to raise money for charity

I love giving a massage – my technique is gentle and relaxing

7 FINISHING OFF A SESSION

I prefer giving my clients extra time at the end to regain their balance. A few minutes are needed for them to come back to the reality of life slowly.

I have had people snoring, which is ok as it shows they had a deep relaxing session. Those who do not wake up, say after 10-20 minutes, I gently whisper for them to come back to life. It's interesting to see them coming back to reality because it's as if they had travelled to a different planet.

After my client has completely regained consciousness, has dressed and is in control, we discuss whether more sessions are required and make bookings in advance if possible.

Essential oils continue to work even a few hours later. Therefore, it's best to advise clients not to wash them off immediately. They must however drink plenty of water to help their body wash out toxins. My massage sessions are designed for complete relaxation so heavy long-distance drive afterwards is not advisable.

I thank my clients for allowing me to be part of their journey, for the wonderful stories they shared with me.

I thank all my spirit guides for helping me connect spiritually with my clients.

The other day my client couldn't stop looking at me, he said:

"That was out of this world! It was the best experience I have ever had!"

Of all the massages in his life, this was by far the best according to his description.

Being part of my client's experience is a wonderful feeling and I always feel honoured. This particular client also loved his feet being massaged. As soon as I touched them he started groaning with pleasure. Even though he kept quiet during the session, when we came to the feet he told me how great it felt, how he loved my touch and how he loved the way I massaged his whole body particularly his feet.

Finally, I thank God and the Universe for aligning everything. I have unwavering faith and I know that they have my back and everything I ask is given. I ask for more joy, prosperity and fulfilment. My life is filled with wealth and success therefore I already feel RICH which is super!

I am grateful that I am given this opportunity to serve humanity. I have found my purpose and it truly makes me happy. The more I focus on my true happiness and my satisfaction, the more I am able to help everyone around me.

After clients leave, I pull out my notebook (client log) and immediately write down everything I have gathered about them. This helps me remember what I need to know about them next time we meet.

I make sure I release any negative energy I might have accumulated during the session. I come out of my therapy room a different person so I reset my thermostat to the level it was before entering the room.

PART 3: MY CLIENTS

8 CLIENT TESTIMONIALS

I have happy clients who are always glad to leave positive feedback on my various online platforms. I love my clients! Here are some of the unedited quotes which illustrate their perspectives so very well:

"You made me so relaxed I felt like I was floating in space!"

"You have the touch of an Angel . . . you took me to heaven and back!"

"You´re even more beautiful in person than you are in that stunning picture of you in that little blue dress!"

"Great body massage - next time I want the foot pampering too!"

"I´m floating on air after that foot massage you gave me yesterday!"

"I loved the way you greeted me with a glowing smile and proceeded to melt away my cares until I glowed inside too!"

"That´s the best massage I´ve ever had in my entire life!"
"WOW!! Boi was sooooo good I was unable to perform normally and didn´t come down from the cloud she took me to until 5 hours after my massage from heaven."

"I biked down from Oxford to be seen to by this lady and will be doing it again and again and again ..."

"Boi apologized after our last session because of the loud noise from the men who had turned up unexpectedly to saw down a nearby tree. I had no idea what she was talking about!"

"I was planning to see you again next week, but I just had to see you tonight!"

"I drive from Kent every weekend to see this gorgeous lady for 3 hours - believe me she is well worth the journey!"

"Amazing massage from a lovely woman! So relaxed afterwards. Thanks again and I´ll be seeing you very very soon. X"

"Lovely girl, great massage. Just switch off, relax & enjoy. Thanks"

"A lovely lady, a fantastic massage, highly recommended"

"A wonderful experience and will return thank you x"

"An excellent service from a very professional lady - highly recommended"

"Punctual, clean room with good facilities, gorgeous girl and stunning service"

"Very nice lady very particular - I like that"

"Incredible pampering experience!"

"Excellent massage just what I needed after a busy weekend, highly recommend"

"You're a lovely lady, thank you so much. Looking forward to my next visit x"

"I would gladly recommend this service if you want to reinvigorate your tired body brilliant massage"

"Once again, a lovely experience, with a lovely young lady"

"My second visit to Boi and even better than the first. She is stunning, friendly, genuine and creates a wonderfully sensuous and relaxing atmosphere xxx"

"Superb...brilliant masseuse...will go again"

"Very professional, very skilled, very friendly. A delightful experience. I am happy to recommend booking this charming lady."

"Beautiful, intelligent, charming lady. A wonderful experience. Will I return? Oh yes!"

"Would definitely visit again... brilliantly relaxing massage"

"I had a fantastic time and will book again X"

"Simply fantastic!"

"I have visited before and for the second time had an hour of pleasure EXCELLENT MASSAGE thank you xx"

"Again, an excellent service from a very professional lady. Highly recommended."

"A lovely experience. I will return soon. Thank you x"

"Boi is a lovely sensitive Lady I had a great relaxing massage And was floating on air by the end. I will be back, thank you"

"She is a real delight - everything perfect, have a good hol - CU in June."

"On time, Boi knows her massage technique and uses it very effectively."

"Boi is Amazing, made me feel wonderful – thank you so much"
"Clean quiet discrete pad, really knows her trade, will definitely book again thanx Princess!"

"Boi is very intelligent ultra-sexy and gives the best service ever. She takes total care and make certain you are totally satisfied. Thanks Boi I will be back!"

"This was one of the best experiences I have ever had, this girl is a gem, Thank you very much for a very pleasant massage."

"An excellent and professional massage service. Highly recommended and very relaxing!"

"Went for longer session. Massage brilliant. Still not long enough with the lovely Boi."

"Wonderful relaxing massage in a very pleasant setting - hope to get back soon"

"Wow - what a massage, an absolute delight. Boi relaxes and excites at the same time. Fantastic!!"

"Thank you so much for such a wonderful time. I never thought it could but it gets better each time I see you"

"Easy friendly booking. Very pleasant room with shower also available. State of the art massage table. I had a massage which was just perfect."

"Boi was very friendly and I immediately felt relaxed. The service was as expected and left me wanting more - I should have booked for a longer session!"

"VERY FRIENDLY, AND FELT VERY COMFORTABLE, AND TOTALLY RELAXED, WOULD BOOK AGAIN. THANK YOU BOI"

"Great service, wonderful massage I can highly recommend her."

"Very good massage, friendly and stunning, highly recommended"

"The best massage I have ever had, treat her with respect guys!!"

"On arrival she had a nice smile, was made welcome. She offered a drink had a chat for only a while, then I had one of the best massage´s ever."

"This lady is unforgettable, thank you so much darling see you again soon"

"Had a fantastic time with a very beautiful lady :-) Cannot wait for next time - thank you x"

PART 4: MY PASSIONS

Giving a massage is not the only thing I am passionate about. I love dancing and modelling is my hobby.

9 DANCING

My love for dancing started when I was in primary school. I liked watching people who were good at dancing and then I would imitate them. For some reason I never joined any dance clubs during my school years. I must have been busy with other things. But by the time I was in secondary school I formed my own after school traditional dance club. I co-ordinated a group of enthusiastic girls eager to dance! We went around performing for locals for free. It was never about making money but rather something interesting to do. I kept the records (eg: attendances, performances, any gifts we collected)

Some of these young girls could sing as well so we formed a mini-choir. Life really was great in those days!

My group practised every day after school and during weekends. We did all our rehearsals outside in the open near my house. Neighbours would gather to watch, and we liked that a lot. My girls enjoyed showing off their skills and talents. Their parents were appreciative as this gave their kids something to do instead of being mischievous somewhere else.

I felt good, so I was always there for them. I was their big sister and they respected me a lot.

The first school at which I started teaching appointed me the school Latin dance coordinator as well as modelling coordinator. I had already leaned some Latin dance (ballroom, cha-cha-cha, jive, quick step, rumba, & samba) during my National Service experience as an assistant teacher so when the post arose I jumped at the chance. I danced with my students and improved my skills. I travelled around the country with my students for competitions and I had a lot of fun.

Dancing became part of my exercise routine, I preferred it rather than going to the gym because it felt perfect for me.

When I moved to London I continued with my dance passion. I joined the local dance scenes. I did some ballroom dancing but when I discovered salsa, I loved it even more! I got hooked because it was so exciting. The dance floor took me to a different planet. I learnt other street Latin dances such as merengue, bachata and kizomba.

My dance group in the early 90's

With my Latin Dance Club students from LSSS

Salsa dancing

Dancing kizomba at a big club in central London

10 MODELLING

Beauty has always fascinated me. I am an artistic person who always sees the beauty in everyone. I believe we are all beautiful in our own way. I loved my students and I became the school Modelling club coordinator at LSSS.

I organised beauty pageants, fashion shows, photo-shoots and together we learnt everything to do with beauty and modelling.

Beauty pageants are competitions of excellence: emphasising dignity, courage, intelligence, humility and kindness. They boost confidence and self-esteem. My beauty queens/kings and I got involved with community projects and we raised money for charities.

I trained catwalk models for beauty pageants and fashion shows.

In London I did some modelling jobs and entered modelling competitions & beauty pageants. I continued organising beauty pageants, trained beauty queens and I became one of the most respected people in the industry.

I continued training models back in Botswana each time I visited. I launched and supported charity projects with some of my beauty queens.

Some of my trainees have been so totally transformed that giving back to humanity is now part of their DNA.

As a former beauty queen, a model trainer and a coach, it is important for me to look after my body. I am a big fan of complementary medicine and believe that natural beauty is the best.

I encourage my models to look after their body. We should look healthy because this increases our confidence and self-esteem. There are so many natural remedies we can use to help us look and feel good about ourselves.

Models in particular must maintain beautiful skin, hair and nails. Their dietary and lifestyle habits are vital.

To prevent problems such as premature aging, dark bags under the eye, chipping nails, skin blemishes & other skin conditions, dry cracking lips, dull hair and bloating belly we must take necessary steps to look after our bodies. Improving your physical appearance will improve your emotional well-being.

Here are my top health tips:
1. Eat small portions of healthy food
2. Drink lots of water
3. Exercise regularly
4. Sleep well
5. Care for your skin
6. Have regular massage therapy
7. Avoid too much caffeine and alcohol

You are what you eat as they say. Eating the right portions of food at the right time is a great way of making sure your meals are balanced.

It's important to feel great inside and out. Your energy level will increase, therefore boosting your mood, brightening your life experience, improving your immune system which helps to clear ailments like headaches, stress related diseases and depression.

The benefits of drinking plenty of water are many. Pure water can help you stay slim, boost your energy and keep you healthy. Your body and brain cannot function properly if you allow yourself to become dehydrated.

Regular exercise promotes general health. It relaxes our body, releases tension in our muscles, calms us and makes us feel happy. Everyone should include it in their everyday routines, not just models!

Good sleep helps prevent wrinkles & inflammations, stimulates muscle growth and inhibits fat production. Aim for seven to eight hours of beauty sleep every day.

Avoid eating just before bed time: eat your dinner at least four hours before bed time and snacks at least two hours before bed time.

Wash your face every evening before bed time to remove dirt and make-up. This will reduce dryness, oiliness or rashes. Moisturise your skin after having a bath. Your skin is renewing itself while you sleep. Give it a boost by providing it with lots of moisture before you go to bed.

Including regular massage therapy, reflexology and aromatherapy in your life will improve peacefulness to the body and mind. The feeling of touch relaxes the whole body, therefore improving well-being. You could go for a head massage, a facial massage, a foot massage or a whole-body massage, whichever suites your style.

Massage has profound effects: it improves circulation, relaxes muscles, aids digestion and speeds up elimination of waste products.

Drinking too much caffeine or alcohol can reduce your ability to sleep well. I always advice my models to avoid them or to minimise their intake if they must consume them.

My daughter Katrinah and I were featured in the book – Complementary Medicine, Beauty and Modelling by Agata Listowska and Mark Nicholson.

One of the pictures of me in the book

Katrinah's featured pictures

As the reigning Mrs Commonwealth, I was invited to the Commonwealth Reception in 2013 given at Buckingham Palace by The Queen and The Duke of Edinburgh. This was the biggest highlight of my modelling journey. It was such a privilege to shake the hand of Her Majesty the Queen who remarked: "I'm a queen of the Commonwealth too!"

How I Got RICH Doing What I LOVE!

A selection of photos from my biography

Article in Fabulos Magazine

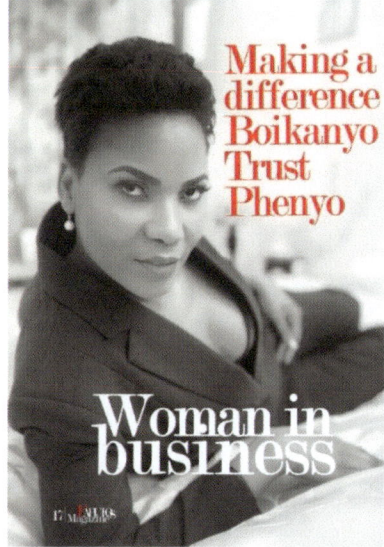

Photo credit: Ali Haydar Yeşilyurt

Photo credit: Ali Yeşilyurt

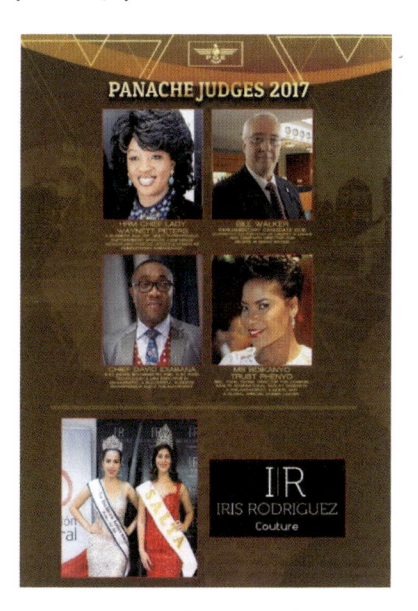

Photo credit: Jay Pedram

Guest on the Pauline Long Show on BEN TV

Photo credits: Ali Haydar Yeşilyurt

Support for Cancel Cancer Africa

Photo credit: Ali Haydar Yeşilyurt

Guest on the Stardust Show

Photo credit: Ali Haydar Yeşilyurt

Portrait

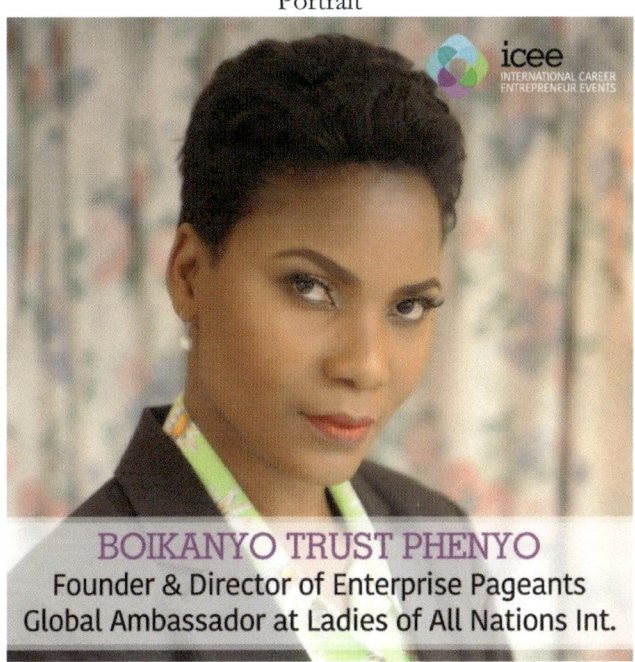

Photo credit: Ali Haydar Yeşilyurt

Miss Commonwealth International 2012 – Miss Teen, Miss & Mrs

Photo credit: Richard Barker

Speaking at Pre-women Economic forum hosted by Justina Mutale Foundation for Leadership

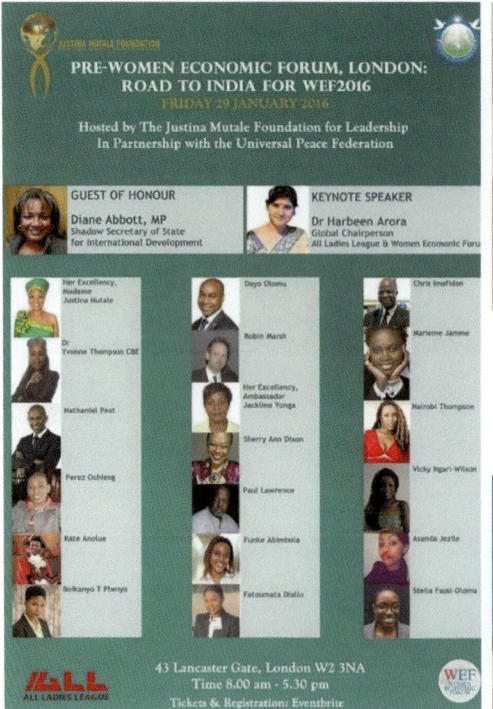

Photo credit: Josh Daniels

My make-up artist Izabela Jung and my Director Lloyd Barrett

Photo credit: Ali Haydar Yeşilyurt

Photo credit: Vladimir Neshkov

The voice Newspaper article

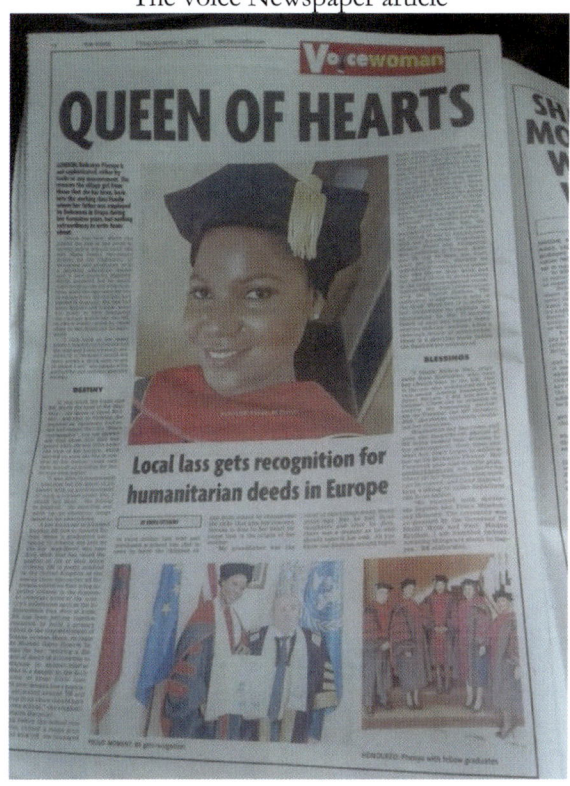

Photoshoot with Janusz Miarka

Fashion Show (Photo credit: Andres Moya)

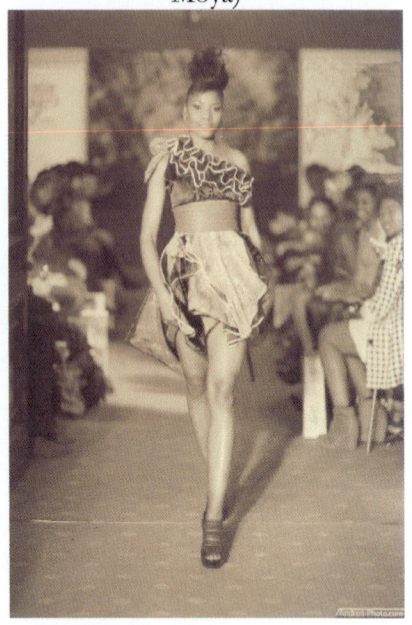

Mrs Commonwealth Internatonal 2012

Photoshoot with Steve Spurgin

Botswana Community UK - Independence event

Botswana Community UK – another Independence event

Photo credit: Mr Gee photography

Photo credit: Lpi photography

Botswana Community UK - Independence event

Photo credit: Photo Miarka

Honorary Doctorate Award

LOANI Expertise book

Peace Missionary Award

A selection with my Beauty Queens

Jessica Martins, Angelica Caye Casinto

Katrinah Phenyo

Nicole Gaelebale, Jessica Dos Santos

Portia Sam

Photo credits: Jay Pedram, Edwin Hwera

Ritah George

Sofia F Rocha

Contestants for Miss Africa GB

World of Beauty Models

Photo credits: BenDan Photography

PGRAE Award (Photo credit: Janusz Miaka)

Massage Therapy Course graduates (Photo: Janusz Miarka)

PART 5: YOU CAN GET RICH TOO!

11 WORK ON YOUR DREAMS

If you don't work on your dreams you will spend your life working on someone else's dream.

Believe it or not you are already equipped to do what needs to be done, you just need to marshal your resources, develop that money-making idea you have had in your mind for ages, make some plans and then just get on with it!

To create every success in your life, what you must do is:
1. Decide to take action
2. Develop a positive mental attitude
3. Believe in your own ability and worthiness

a) Getting rich is an inside job

Start with you! Love yourself. Appreciate your worth. Everything in your life will work out the minute you decide to love yourself enough to stop the pain you are suffering.

You are what you constantly think about so recognize the value of your thoughts. What do you think of when you think of being rich? Your current thinking can either hold you back or propel you forward towards experiencing greater riches in your life. Replace negative painful thoughts that do not serve you with positive pleasant thoughts that do. Train your mind and be in control.

Improve your willpower through imagination. Imagination is such a powerful thing, but you need to utilize it in a positive way. Create a clear vision of richness. For example: "I will be a millionaire by the age of 40!" What do you want to create in your life and in this world? Define a vision of your future self.

The only person you need to please is yourself. Do not live by anyone else's standards. Set your own and live by them. Do it for yourself, not for recognition. Continue to work on impressing yourself. Focus on intrinsic motivation and drive because these come from within. Do things that make you feel good. Personal satisfaction connects you with your personal values. Own your uniqueness. There is nobody like you in the world so be very proud of who you really are.

Get in the habit of rewarding yourself. You have greatness within you.

b)   Set your goals

"Setting goals is the first step in turning the invisible into the visible" ~ Tony Robbins ~

Change your life by making new decisions to start a new life. Creating your future is not something that happens to you, but it is something that you decide to happen!

Your goals should be personal so write them down. Be specific and choose what you want to focus on. Choose to become something more. Identify and learn to accept your own set of talents, skills, strengths, creativity and knowledge. Set your mind to achieve greatness. There is nothing you cannot do, be or have!

Goals are crucial at steering you in the right direction. Have clear effective, smart and time bound goals. Focus on where you want to go, not on what you fear might stop you going there.

Energy follows thought. Therefore, where your focus goes, energy follows. Follow your passion because it is the fuel to motivation. But for motivation to last, you must genuinely love and enjoy what you are doing.

Do you know what brings you joy? Do you know what really puts a smile on your face and makes you happy?

Spend time and effort on the things that truly make you feel good and trust your instincts. Your mind has been designed to guide you in the right direction and align with who you really are so listen to it. This should help you find your purpose on this planet. Remember, the universe has your back always so be still and know that all is well. Your ultimate objective is to become the best version of yourself that you can be.

Spend your quality time defining your goals and what you really want? I use easy-to-use tools like vision board, affirmations and mind mapping to draw and define my goals. Trust me they work! My life is rich in value, meaning and purpose. I wish this to be so for you too.

Figure out the "What" and the "Why" and the "How" will reveal itself.

c)   Consistency is key

Consistency builds habit. You are what you repeatedly do.

Grow to become the person that matches your goals. Have an

accountability partner, a mentor to keep you on the right track. It's easy to slip back and continue living someone else's dream. Wake up and do the little things or habits that will lead you to your greater self.

It's so easy. Once you figure out it isn't hard!

But understand that along the way there will be obstacles and problems. Problems give rise to growth. Allow yourself to make mistakes. Nobody is perfect. Learn from your mistakes and let them go.

Taking a risk is the beginning of the process. Do not be afraid of being out of your comfort zone. Most rewards come from taking risks.

Every master has been a disaster. Therefore, if you want to make a difference in this world you have to have the motivation and passion to overcome all obstacles between you and your vision for your future. Pain is part of that journey.

Be determined to succeed. Be patient. Keep going. Never give up until you have reached your goals.

d) The secret of living rich

I believe that true and lasting happiness is never the result of how much money you have in the bank.

You are already rich. Look at everything that you have. Count your blessings. Give thanks and be grateful. When you are grateful, fear disappears and abundance appears.

The more you focus on those areas where you are already wealthy, the more you will realize how rich you already are. Knowing that what you choose to focus on becomes your reality will help you figure out how easy life can be!

Our entire experience on this planet is determined by how we choose to perceive our reality, so become more aware of your surroundings, of what you say to yourself and what you focus on all day long.

Most importantly, live life, enjoy life, be free and be happy!

Stay true to yourself. Never compromise your self-identity. Love yourself.

Forgive everything and everybody.

Choose love. The force of love is the most powerful force on Earth. Radiate love to everything that you do and everybody that you meet.

Give back, serve the community. Although we may live separate lives, we are all connected. Your life will have a true meaning when you contribute to the lives of others.

PART 6: WHAT DO EXPERTS SAY

12 QUOTES FROM SUCCESSFUL PEOPLE

Do what you love, and you will never work again.
~ Ed J C Smith ~
Founder, Champion Academy

See what you want, get what you see.
~Jack Canfield ~
Motivational speaker

To achieve great success in business you have to have an outrageously rich vision.
~ Sol Kerzner ~
Billionaire hotelier

You've got to be a believer in what you do.
~ Sir Philip Green ~
Retail billionaire

If you want to feel rich, just count the things you have that money can't buy.
~ Old proverb ~

You can start out with nothing, and out of nothing, and out of no way, a way will be made.
~ Michael Bernard Beckwith ~
Spiritual enthusiast

It is one of the beautiful compensations in this life that no one can sincerely try to help another without helping himself.
~ Ralph Waldo Emerson ~

Surrender to what is. Say "yes" to life and see how life suddenly starts working for you, rather than against you.
~ Eckhart Tolle ~
Author

The real source of wealth and capital in this new era is not material things. It is the human mind, the human spirit, the human imagination, and our faith in the future.
~ Steve Forbes ~
Billionaire publisher

No one can make you inferior without your consent.
~ Eleanor Roosevelt ~
First lady of the United States

In order to kick ass, you must first lift up your foot.
~ Jen Sincero ~
Author

One of the top tips for becoming wealthy is to set a goal. Write it down, make a plan and learn everything you possibly can, then go to work really hard but be flexible and prepared to make changes.
~ Brian Tracy ~
Top business and personal success speaker

I have lived a long life and had many troubles, most of which never happened.
~ Mark Twain ~
Author

Change your mindset from scarcity to sufficiency to Abundance!
~ D C Cordova ~
CEO, Money & You

Humans can do the most remarkable things no matter what.
~ Jim Rohn ~
Motivational speaker

Most people who grow rich do it methodically, strategically. They have patience and look at the long term. Long term vision pays - instant gratification costs.
~ John Demartini ~
Founder, Demartini Institute

Trust your inner voice – it will give you feedback on what needs to be learnt.
~ Cappi Pidwell ~
Well-known speaker

A good work-life balance is a good indicator of whether someone is truly happy and fulfilled or whether they are controlled by the demands of life.
~ Hannah Bontle Lecha ~
Founder, Leadership Nurturing

Believe in your talents and improve them to bring even more pleasure to the many who also believe and even less to the few who don't!
~ Philip Wake ~
IT expert

If you think you will get wealthy just through visualization you are kidding yourself. Consistent, persistent and inspired action is required. Diligent consistency to take massive action again and again and again!
~ John Spencer Ellis ~
Fitness billionaire

Becoming rich isn't just about piling up the money. Far from it. To be successful these days, you need to be rich in happiness, friendships, health and ideas.
~ Sir Richard Branson ~
Founder, Virgin group

You need to start YOUR own personal journey to RICHES and the time to start – is NOW!
~ Gill Fielding ~
Self-made millionaire

So why do some people become richer than others when they have the same background and same opportunities? Well it is all down to the value that someone has instilled inside of themselves. If they have an innate ability to SEE the value of who they are they can see that value to have more money and more of anything they want.
~ Nicole Brandon ~
Author

Sharing your life is where riches start happening!
~ Marie Diamond ~
Top transformational leader

Being rich is living your life on your own terms – according to your possibilities, not your limitations.
~ Paul Mckenna ~
Hypnotist & author

Passions keep evolving. Follow them because this is where you will find your greatest success and the most you can make and the legacy you will leave!
~ Gary Goldstein ~
Hollywood film producer

So, if you and I want to achieve greater financial success we must align any action with who we are.
~ Peter Thomson ~
Leading strategist on business and personal growth

If you are going to be successful in any way, there is one thing you must do… Follow your heart! Ignore all of the noise around you, go inside and listen to what your heart tells you. You will have every success you've dreamed of.
~ Woody Woodward ~
Founder, The Law of Importance

When thinking of setting goals, you are either in charge of your dreams or a tool of someone else's.
~ Topher Morrison ~
Creator of Music Trance series

The best time to start a business is NOW! There is never a perfect time and if you wait for it – it will never happen. Start now! Procrastination is the death of opportunity.
~ Jonathan Jay ~
Founder, The coaching Academy

The biggest lesson I learnt in business is the importance of consistency and constancy. If you have a plan that is written, and you focus on it inevitably things will go wrong. At this point don't lose sight of your goals – you need to find solutions. If you go off the rails, miss your target or start to drift you must get back on track and stay on track.
~ James Caan ~
Entrepreneur, TV personality

Wealth is what you have left when you have lost all of your money. Money is temporary, it is only ink on paper. Wealth is permanent. It is your network, your skill sets, your passion, your resources and your talents and your reputation. It is all of the intangible stuff, so if you want more money start by increasing your wealth.
~ Bruce Muzik ~
Founder, Designer Life

You are never alone or helpless. The force that guides the stars guides you too.
~ Shrii Shrii Anandamurti ~
Indian philosopher

If you are depressed, you are living in the past. If you are anxious, you are living in the future. If you are at peace, you are living in the present.
~ Lao Tzu ~
Founder, Taoism

Failing to plan is planning to fail.
~ Robert Schuller ~
Christian televangelist

PART 7: RESOURCES

MY VIDEOS

If you would like to see more of my massage work, please visit my YouTube channel, while you are there, please help me by subscribing and giving my videos a like as this will encourage me to do more: www.youtube.com/channel/UCSt4M4L88Pe9z9JJo-OrwLw

Keep up-to date with what I am doing on Facebook:
www.facebook.com/btphenyo
www.facebook.com/princessboikanyo

BOOKS I HAVE READ

I love reading and my library of books increases all the time. Books give me the inspiration I need daily. I learn from the best teachers out there who have walked the path before me. Here is a list of my favorites. Do check them out:

1. The Secret by Rhonda Byrne
2. Ask and it Is Given: Learning to Manifest your Desires by Gerry, Ester & Abraham Hicks
3. The Dynamic Laws of Prosperity by Catherine Ponder

4. Think and Grow Rich by Napoleon Hill
5. The Power of Your Subconscious Mind by Joseph Murphy
6. The Strangest Secret by Earl Nightingale
7. Outliers: The Story of Success by Malcolm Gladwell
8. The Richest Man in Babylon by George S Clason
9. Skill with People by Les Giblin
10. Challenge to Succeed CD Program by Jim Rohn
11. The Science of Getting Rich by Wallace D Wattles
12. Women Who Love Too Much: When You Keep Wishing and Hoping He'll Change by Robin Norwood
13. The Magic of Thinking Big by David Schwartz
14. The Best of Les Brown Audio Collection by Les Brown
15. The Complete Book of Massage by Clare Maxwell-Hudson
16. Complementary Medicine: Beauty and Modelling by Agata A Listowska & Mark A Nicholson
17. Secrets of the Millionaire Mind: Mastering the Inner Game of Wealth by T Harv Eker
18. Riches: The 7 Secrets of Wealth You Were Never Told by Gill Fielding
19. How to Stop Worrying and Start Living by Dale Carnegie
20. I Can Make You Rich by Paul McKenna
21. You are a Badass: How to Stop Doubting Your Greatness and Start Living an Awesome Life by Jen Sincero
22. Behind Her Brand: Expert Edition by Kimberly Pitts
23. Power to Succeed by Elliot Kay
24. The Success Principles by Jack Canfield
25. Rich Dad Poor Dad: What the Rich Teach Their Kids About Money… by Robert Kiyosaki
26. Starts with You: The who-wants-to-be-perfect-anyway approach to experiencing more fulfilling relationships by Rebecca Miller
27. The 7 Habits of Highly Effective People: Powerful Lessons in Personal Change by Stephen R Covey
28. The 21 Irrefutable Laws of Leadership by John C Maxwell
29. Unshakable: Your Financial Freedom Playbook by Tony Robbins
30. Good Leaders Ask Great Questions: Your Foundation for Successful Leadership by John C Maxwell
31. The 4-hour Work Week by Timothy Ferriss
32. Questions are the Answers by Allan Pease
33. The life lessons & rules for success by Anthony Robbins
34. How to Win Friends & Influence People by Dale Carnegie

35. The Compound Effect by Darren Hardy
36. The Greatest Secret in the World by Og Mandino
37. Secrets about Men every Woman Should Know by Barbara De Angelis
38. Motivation in 7 Simple Steps by Marta Tuchowska
39. Speak so Your Audience Will Listen by Robin Kermode
40. Passive Income Bible by Kazi Jackson
41. Bitcoin the Future of Money by Dominic Frisby
42. Success, it's as Simple as ABC by David Hannon
43. 1001 ways to Get more Customers by Chris Cardell & Jonathan Jay
44. Eleven Miles by Lance Greenfield
45. SUPERgirl 2 SUPERwoman by Sheun Oke
46. The Youth Evolution by Yetunde Adeshile
47. The Complete Beauty Book by Helena Sunnydale
48. Smiles from Around the World by Ingrid Marn
49. Being a Model, Second Edition by Roshumba Williams with Anne Marie O'Connor
50. Making a Supermodel: A Parent's Guide by Janice Celeste
51. The Power of Positive Energy by Adrian Teodoro
52. Money Mindfulness Daily: What School Failed to Teach You by Ed J C Smith
53. Scientific Healing Affirmations by Paramahansa Yogananda
54. The Power of Now by Eckhart Tolle
55. Mindfulness pocketbook by Gill Hasson
56. Feel the Fear and Do it Anyway by Susan Jeffers
57. I Can Make You Happy by Paul McKenna
58. Solving the Property Puzzle by Gill Fielding
59. Solving the Financial Success Puzzle by Gill Fielding
60. The Memoirs of Enole Ditsheko by Enole Ditsheko
61. I Selfie, Therefore I AM: The Metamorphoses of The Self in The Digital Era by Elsa Godart
62. A Beginners Guide to Pendulum Dowsing by Brenda Hunt
63. Start Late, Finish Rich: A No-Fail Plan for Achieving Financial Freedom at Any Age by David Bach
64. E-Myth Revisited: Why Most Small Businesses Don't Work and What to Do About It by Michael E. Gerber
65. How to Sell a Business by Jacob Orosz
66. How to Buy and Sell Great Businesses: How to Find, Fund, Fix and Flip Businesses for Profit by Jonathan Jay
67. The Seven Spiritual Laws of Success by Deepak Chopra

68. Bitcoin: The Rise of New Money by James Hamilton

ABOUT THE AUTHOR

A Brief Biography of
Dr Boikanyo Trust Phenyo BSc, PGDE, PGDSE

Born in a remote village in Botswana 11 miles from the nearest school, Boikanyo showed her determination to succeed from an early age by running the full distance every school-day and arriving on time without fail. The fitness she achieved enabled her to win races and study hard so nobody was surprised when she got a place at university in the capital, graduated with honours and went on to gain her masters in the teaching of Mathematics & Physics.

After working as a teacher in Letlhakane Senior Secondary School in Botswana for four years and getting involved in the modelling & beauty pageant business she decided it was time to expand her horizons and moved to the UK and over the following ten years became a successful modelling & beauty queen consultant. Every year she helped organise the celebration of Botswana Independence day in London and returned to her home village to provide support in the form of clothes and Christmas party for the kids who no longer have to walk to school because her 5-year project to raise funds for a school bus came to fruition in December 2014.

In 2016 the 50th Golden Jubilee of Botswana Independence Day which she organised included her appearing on the BBC documentary Black and British – A forgotten History – Episode 4 when a plaque honouring the 3 kings who persuaded Queen Victoria to protect Botswana against the political ambitions of South Africa was installed at the Botswana High Commission in London.

Gaining the title Mrs Commonwealth International 2012, Boikanyo became deeply involved in the activities of a beauty pageant which uniquely empowers its title holders to run charitable projects for the benefit of their home country. She attended charitable events as one of the triple queens (Miss Teen, Miss & Mrs), provided catwalk training for the finalists, ran workshops for the title holders to ensure that they understood their roles & objectives, acted as their personal consultant and was appointed Director of Events & Projects in 2014. She organized support for the website and Facebook page which was essential to attract contestants, promote activities and report on the successful achievements of the title holders.

Boikanyo was proud to be the recipient of various awards including: Empowering African Women in Europe Award 2013, African Achievers Award 2013, Panache Global Recognition & Award for Excellence 2014, International Achievers Award (IAA) 2014, Top 100 Outstanding Africans Making a Difference 2015, Best Motivational Role Model 2015, Outstanding Supporting Judge 2015, Lifetime Achievement award from the

IAA 2016, Ladies Of All Nations International Global Ambassador (LOANI) award 2016 & 2017.

She has become a well known personality who was excited to meet & become ongoing friends with the Botswana athletes at the London Olympic Village in 2012. She was honoured to meet the royal family at the Commonwealth of Nations Reception at Buckingham Palace in 2013 and, was interviewed on various TV shows in 2015-16 including Princess Halliday, Chrissy B, Pauline Long and Sporah. She has appeared in various publications including an interview with Touch Base Africa and an article about her Making a Difference in Fabulos Magazine in 2018. She has been a catwalk choreographer and guest judge at numerous beauty pageants including Miss Commonwealth, Miss England Rugby, Miss Portugal UK, Miss London Borough, Miss Africa GB, Miss Southern Africa UK and many more.

This lady has inspired everybody she met including the author Lance Greenfield who wrote a book that she edited called Eleven Miles about an amazing lady who had to run 11 miles to school every day and overcame all the odds to graduate from university and become a successful Olympic athlete!

Boikanyo was very proud to be appointed by Justina Mutale in 2014 as the Botswana representative for Positive Runway Red Ribbon Models and in 2016 a committee member of the Justina Mutale Foundation for Leadership. She was also proud to be appointed by Ikanyeng Moipolai as International Representative in Europe for the award winning Destiny Organisation in 2016.

Boikanyo is much in demand as a public speaker. She has been a motivational guest speaker at numerous events including the Pauline Long Show on BEN TV, the Elutec Academy of Design and Engineering, Frederick Bremer School, Blog Talk Radio, Stardust Radio, Every Woman Matters UK Summit, Mma Mosadi Movement Maun Women Empowerment and the 2017 International Career & Entrepreneur Event.

Boikanyo continues to empower African women everywhere to achieve their rightful place in the world. She is proud to be part of the Justina Mutale Foundation for Leadership which launched a Scholarship Programme in 2016, to be International Representative in Europe for the Destiny Organisation which received several awards in 2016 for its outstanding contributions to humanity and to be one of the global ambassadors for LOANI. She looks forward to the exciting challenges that the future with these inspirational organisations will bring.

Boikanyo is a successful massage therapist whose magic fingers and healing hands were uniquely accompanied by counselling skills which together with her model training and beauty pageant consultant experience have lead to her becoming a Lifestyle Specialist who works with people who want to improve their lifestyles through: relaxation (massage), healthy eating (diet & nutrition), fitness (yoga & exercise) and counselling (mostly relationship). In 2017 she decided it was time to share her skills with women in her home country Botswana and organised massage training as a way of encouraging her fellow country women to start up their own businesses to set them free by becoming masters of their own fate.

For her outstanding contribution in the society Boikanyo was honoured with a doctorate degree by the Academy of Universal Peace in October 2018 in Tirana, Albania. It was at this event where she was also appointed a Peace Missionary by the Diplomatic Mission, Peace and Prosperity.

To celebrate their 10th year anniversary in October 2018, BEFFTA decided to select and honour great personalities who make a huge difference in their communities and Boikanyo was among those specially selected to receive the BEFFTA People's Choice Award 2018. BEFFTA, which stands for (Black Entertainment Film Fashion Television and Arts awards) is Europe's biggest and most prestigious award ceremony which celebrates the achievements of black and ethnic personalities all over the world in entertainment, film, fashion, television, arts, philanthropy, sports and leadership. Previous recipients of BEFFTA Special honorary awards include Sir Trevor McDonald OBE, Sir Lenny Henry CBE, Omotola Jelade Ekeinde, Quincy Jones, Tyler Perry, Diane Abbott, Lord John Bird and many more well-known personalities. This was therefore a prestigious award which Boikanyo was surprised and delighted to have received.

Visit her websites at www.boikanyo.com and www.princessboikanyo.org

NOTES

Printed in Great Britain
by Amazon